Queen

SIDE B

1. Liar
2. The Night Comes Down
3. Modern Times Rock 'n' Roll
4. Son and Daughter
5. Jesus
6. Seven Seas of Rhye

QUEEN

QUEEN

The Unauthorized Biography

Written by Soledad Romero Mariño ★ Illustrated by Laura Castelló

1946, ZANZIBAR

Farrokh Bulsara (Freddie Mercury) is born on the distant shores of Zanzibar. In the photo: Freddie Mercury with his little sister, Kashmira.

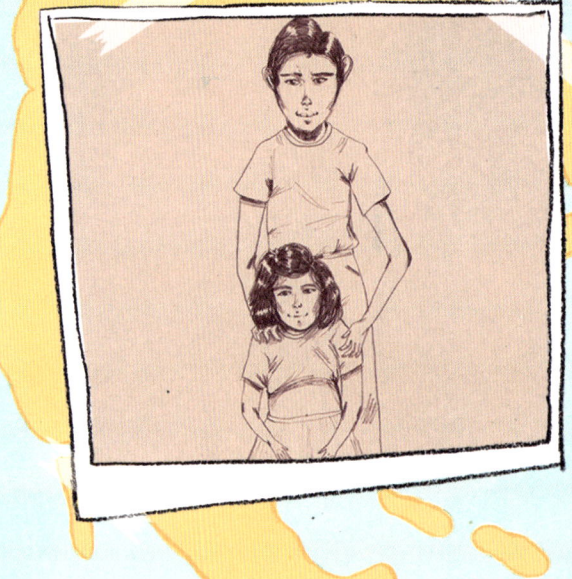

London

1954, BOMBAY

Farrokh travels to Bombay to begin his studies at a British boarding school.

WORLD MAP

1970, LONDON

Freddie Mercury moves to London. Freddie, Brian May, Roger Taylor, and John Deacon form the band Queen.

1974, WORLD TOUR

Queen begins to travel all over the world to promote their music and perform live.

Bombay

Zanzibar

This is where it all started

1946

Freddie Mercury is born in Zanzibar, Tanzania. His parents, Bomi and Jer Bulsara, had moved to Zanzibar from India.

1954

He begins studying at St. Peter's School in Bombay, where he discovers his musical talent.

1965

Freddie and his family move to London.

1966

In art school, Freddie meets Tim Staffell, singer of the band Smile.

1970

Tim leaves Smile and Freddie replaces him. Just like that, a new band is born: Queen.

1971

John Deacon joins Queen as the bassist.

1973

Queen records their first album during the free hours at Trident studios.

1974

The band starts a world tour.

1975

They record "Bohemian Rhapsody." It is considered one of the best songs in the history of rock.

FARROKH BULSARA

Young Farrokh Bulsara landed in Bombay (later known as Mumbai), India, carrying a large suitcase. At the age of eight, he was there to begin his studies at the prestigious St. Peter's School, an English boarding school only for boys of a certain social level.

Farrokh was a shy child. He didn't talk much, but he'd had bright eyes and big dreams ever since he was little. When he laughed—something he did often—his big, crooked teeth looked like they were going to fly off like a flock of frightened seagulls.

At school, he started going by Freddie, an English version of his name. He adapted to his new life, far away from the white sandy beaches and perfumed fields of Zanzibar, the island where his family lived.

HE DIDN'T TALK MUCH,

but he'd had bright eyes and big dreams ever since he was little.

BOMBAY

Freddie was a hardworking student and a good athlete. He played hockey and table tennis, and he also boxed, but his artistic talent shined during a music class. When all the children sang under the direction of the teacher, Freddie's voice stood out.

"He's a child with an extraordinary voice!" murmured the teacher, while his fingers ruffled his mustache. "It would be wonderful if he could take piano lessons…" The professor kept muttering while Freddie left everyone speechless with his singing.

After witnessing such a spectacular performance, the teacher could not wait to finish the class. He shot like a lightning bolt out of the classroom, hurrying through the corridors of the school until he reached the principal's office.

"Freddie is a prodigy!" he repeated wildly, out of breath.

It was not difficult for Freddie's teacher to convince the principal to write to the Bulsara family and ask that Freddie start piano lessons. In addition to singing in the choir, Freddie also performed in plays and played in a rock band with five other friends from school.

His passion for performing would become something unstoppable.

It was easy to imagine that he would never come down from the stage again.

St. Peter's School, 1954

HIS PASSION for performing would become something unstoppable. It was easy to imagine that he would never come down from the stage again.

LONDON, 1965

At age seventeen, Freddie finished his studies in Bombay and returned to Zanzibar with his family. He had become a tall, enthusiastic, and dreamy young man.

But life on the island was no longer safe. The whole family was forced to move. After living in a world of luxury, tranquility, and sun, the Bulsara family now faced the noise, excess, and gray skies of London.

Ealing Art College, 1966

ART CLASSES

London was fashionable, young people ran the streets, and art was everywhere. The shy and innocent Freddie was living in the middle of a bustling city that until then he had only read about in magazines. Something sparked inside of Freddie in this new place. He decided to unleash his inner artist and enrolled in the prestigious Ealing Art College.

Freddie studied design and fashion during the day, singing in some rock bands at night. But it was the band of Tim Staffell, a fellow art school student, that really impressed him.

"Freddie! Tonight we're rehearsing in the theater. Will you come?" shouted Tim as he left the classroom. Freddie could not hide his enthusiasm.

"Count on it!" Freddie replied.

"BOREDOM IS THE BIGGEST DISEASE IN THE WORLD, DARLING."

—Freddie Mercury

The THEATER

The back door of the theater was open. Freddie entered a gallery full of objects: tables, wigs, costumes, lamps. Behind the red velvet curtains, the stage was hidden. Freddie approached shyly, pushed back the curtain, and cleared his throat to make his presence known.

Tim turned around and smiled.

"It is the honorable Freddie," said Tim, bowing. "This is the majestic room where Smile rehearses, courtesy of the great contacts of our genius and guitarist, Brian May."

"Nice to meet you, Freddie," Brian said. He flipped the coin that he had been using to strum the strings of his guitar.

Roger Taylor, the drummer of the band, got up and took a step forward. "Tim has told us a lot about you, Freddie. Welcome, pick a seat." He pointed his drumsticks toward the empty seats in the audience.

Freddie smiled, a little embarrassed by the importance they gave him. He sat in the third row and, almost unblinking, remained motionless during the two-hour rehearsal.

Smile was a great inspiration for Freddie. He followed them to all their concerts.

Smile got to be the opening act at important concerts. The band recorded its first songs and was making its way into the world of music when Tim, to everyone's surprise, announced that he was leaving the band.

It was a great opportunity for Freddie, who was eager to join the group. But first he only needed to convince them.

Brian and Roger met Freddie at his apartment in Kensington, the artist neighborhood where he lived with other students. In the living room, Brian and Roger admired Freddie's incredible collection of records while Freddie selected one by his idol—an unforgettable concert that Jimi Hendrix recorded shortly before his death. The first notes of the master's guitar waving in the room gave Freddie the courage he needed to launch his proposal:

"It would be a great honor for me to replace Tim," Freddie suggested. "I could sing with you."

Brian and Roger shared a knowing look, having already suspected Freddie's intentions. They were well aware not only of his talent in singing but also his great passion for music. He had even advised them on some Smile songs with much success.

"Freddie, you're in," Brian said. He extended his hand to close the deal.

Freddie and Brian shook hands—though the three quickly broke into a big hug. They would start something new—Smile was left behind, and a new band was born in that living room, with the smell of incense in the air and Jimi Hendrix spinning on the turntable.

AN OPPORTUNITY

They
would start
something new—
SMILE
was left behind.

London, 1970

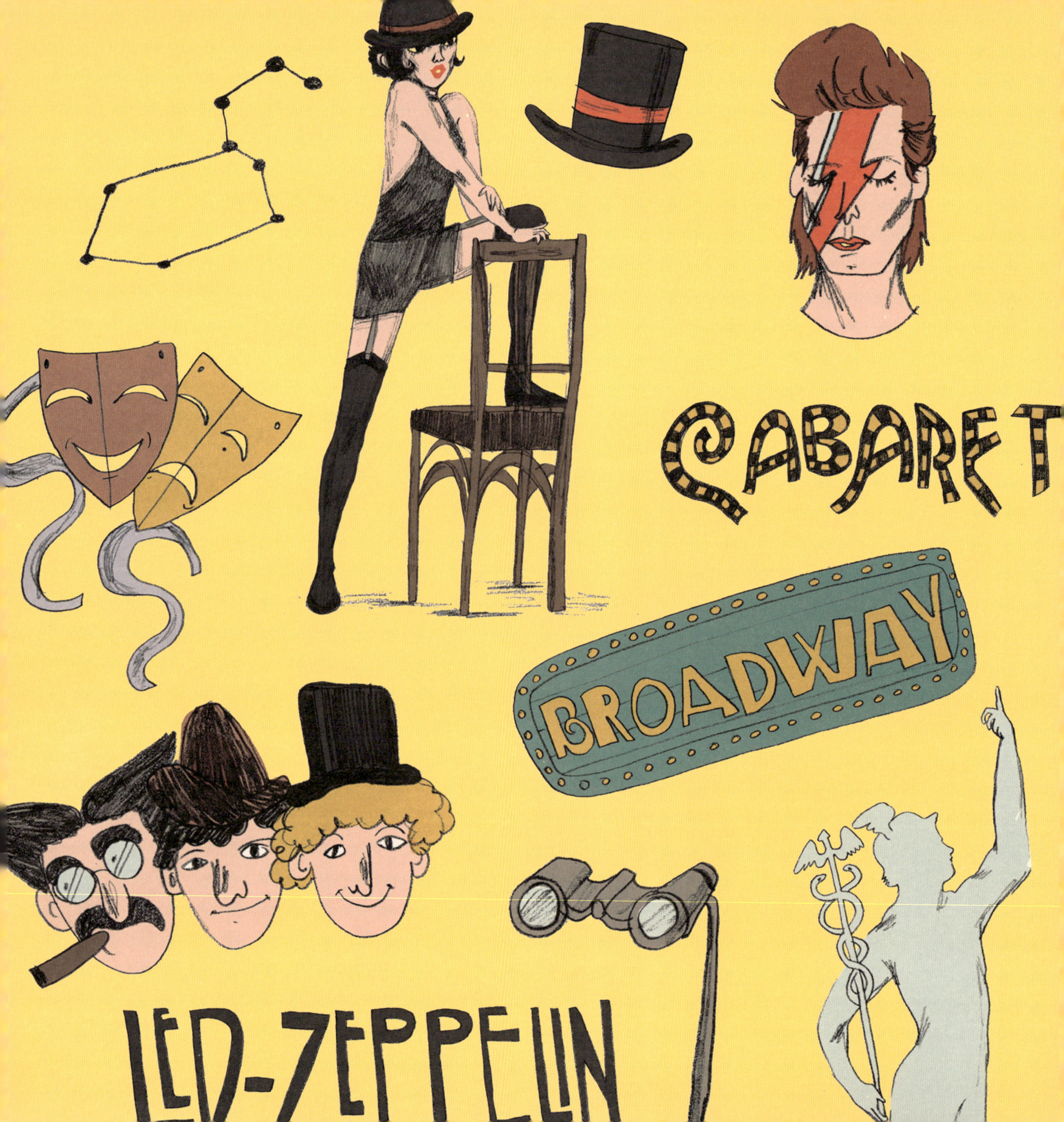

CABARET

BROADWAY

LED-ZEPPELIN

QUEEN

The first thing Freddie, Brian, and Roger did was try to choose a name.

"The Grand Dance," suggested Brian. It was the title of a book, and Brian could not help giving an intellectual touch to everything he did.

"Rich Kids," Roger proposed.

Freddie had other ideas. In fact, only one:

"Queen," Freddie said.

"'Queen' for a band formed by men? I don't get it," Brian replied.

"We have to have an impact and shock right away. We don't want people to have to think about whether they like us or not," Freddie said. "Queen is a powerful, short, and undeniably striking name."

In April 1970, the band Queen began to write the first pages of its history.

REHEARSALS

The rehearsals began. Soon a bass player joined the band. His name was John Deacon, a quiet, modest guy and a phenomenon of electronic music.

It was in those days when Freddie Bulsara became known as Freddie Mercury, the stage name he would use to leave behind his shyness so he could shine onstage.

The four bandmates met in the theater to write and rehearse new songs for countless hours. They looked for an innovative sound, chased the strength of rock, and let the beauty of the theatre inspire them.

"It's not about creating the best music, but about surprising with an unforgettable show. Everything is important: the performance, the effects, the lights, the costumes..." Freddie shouted as he walked the stage from end to end.

Queen aspired to the best, to be different, to be great.

They chased the STRENGTH of rock and let the BEAUTY of the theater inspire them.

THE LINEUP

ROLE IN THE BAND: Singer and composer. Also created the brand of the band.

OFF THE STAGE: His family is from India, but Freddie was born in Zanzibar, the island where his father worked for the British crown.

ONSTAGE: Sings with the top half of a microphone stand. His voice is compared to that of an opera singer.

FUN FACT: Uses a piano as the headboard of his bed. He learns to play lying down and backward, in case inspiration wakes him.

THE LEGEND: He becomes a symbol of gay culture. In the spring of 1987, he is diagnosed with AIDS, an unknown new disease at the time that eventually leads to his death. Freddie continues with music until all his strength is exhausted: the show must go on.

FREDDIE MERCURY
(1946, Zanzibar – 1991, London)

"Labels confuse, they slip me."

ROLE IN THE BAND: Guitarist and composer.

OFF THE STAGE: Passionate about astronomy and earns a PhD in astrophysics.

ONSTAGE: Wears low-key clothes and his iconic white clogs.

FUN FACT: Plays his guitar with sixpence coins, and does not use picks.

THE LEGEND: At sixteen years old, he and his father built an electric guitar from the wood of a Victorian fireplace mantel, an old table, and bicycle saddlebag parts. The famous Red Special continues after decades without going out of tune.

BRIAN MAY
(1947, London)

"The guitar was my weapon, my shield to hide behind."

ROLE IN THE BAND: Drummer, chorus, and composer.

OFF THE STAGE: Biologist and dentist.

ONSTAGE: Next to Freddie, he's one of the most daring members of the band.

FUN FACT: One night, to avoid a fight, he swears that he is a black belt in judo and claims that the law requires him to say it three times before exercising his right to hit his opponents. Roger manages to avoid the fight without knowing the first thing about judo.

THE LEGEND: He locks himself in a closet until Freddie agrees to use "I'm In Love With My Car" as the B side of the "Bohemian Rhapsody" single record. ✲

Records have an A side and a B side. You can play the song on side A, then flip the record over to listen to the song on side B.

ROGER TAYLOR
(1949, King's Lynn, England)

"At the end of it all, there has to be something that makes it worthwhile, even if it's the freedom to do what you want."

ROLE IN THE BAND: Bassist and composer.

OFF THE STAGE: Electronic engineer.

ONSTAGE: In the beginning, Freddie argues with him, since he thinks John's clothes aren't extravagant enough for their performances.

FUN FACT: He is the most unassuming and straightforward in the band, traveling easily on public transportation without being noticed.

THE LEGEND: He is the last member to join the band, and when Freddie dies, he refuses to continue performing with the other members of Queen.

JOHN DEACON
(1951, Leicester, England)

"Arguments are healthy. They clear the air."

"I AM SO POWERFUL ONSTAGE THAT I SEEM TO HAVE CREATED A **MONSTER**. WHEN I'M PERFORMING, I'M *an extrovert*, YET INSIDE I'M A COMPLETELY *different man*."

—Freddie Mercury

THE FIRST SHOW

The four bandmates made sure everything was ready: the instruments, lights, decoration, and clothing. Understandably, everyone was a little nervous.

"Are you going to go out wearing that?" said Freddie, pointing to John's shirt.

"I like it," John replied quietly.

"I think it would be more shocking to wear something like…" Freddie trailed off while rifling through a suitcase full of clothes. Freddie wanted the band to wear extravagant outfits, with leather and diamonds. His bandmates did not agree.

Finally, the young men went on stage, which was not very big and barely fit the four musicians. Between colored lights and a curtain of smoke, the concert began with a happy melody, full of strength and rhythm.

Without a doubt, Brian, Roger, and John were masters with their instruments. Freddie's voice had an indomitable strength. He sang and walked the stage, played with the microphone, and moved his whole body to the rhythm of the music.

Freddie felt happy and reveled in the moment. He shone like a real star. The crowd started getting up from their seats and moved closer to the stage, cheering for each of the songs and the great show the band offered.

"A concert is not a live rendition of our album.
It's a theatrical event."
—FREDDIE MERCURY

RECIPE FOR
QUEEN

AN INTENSE, SOPHISTICATED DISH WITH SURPRISING INGREDIENTS

A lot of classic and popular rock
A bit of heavy metal
A pinch of rockabilly
A few handfuls of dance music
A good dash of pop melodies
Some ballads
Different bits of opera
A touch of blues
A hint of funk

ENJOY IT WITH
A lot of theater
All the glamour you have

"Keep yourself alive."

THEY RECORD THE ALBUM

"Freddie, wake up!"

Freddie sat up, rubbing his eyes, and asked, half-asleep, "What's going on?"

"It's time," said Roger. "We have to go to the recording studio. David"—the great artist, David Bowie—"just finished recording. It's our turn."

Freddie sat up and looked out the window—it was still nighttime. They left for the studio in a hurry.

They had managed to sign a first album, but they had to record in the free hours of the studio. There were long nights. They left the studio at dawn. The streets were deserted and the bandmates were exhausted, but excitement filled their hearts.

WORLD TOUR

Despite the talent of the band, the success came slowly, little by little.

Queen performed their show for the world and managed to record another two albums. Each time they were better.

Their music and audience were growing, but they wanted more.

BOHEMIAN RHAPSODY

They were all gathered in the recording studio, preparing their fourth album. No one could imagine that something like this was possible, except for Freddie, whose head was full of dreams only he had the power to turn into reality.

Freddie was talking fast in front of the piano and trying to explain to his bandmates the crazy idea that kept him from sleeping.

"There are six parts, six styles, six songs…that come together in one great song!"

THE STRUCTURE:
- A CAPPELLA
- INTRODUCTION
- BALLAD
- GUITAR SOLO
- OPERA
- ROCK
- BALLAD AGAIN

Freddie continued before the bewildered gaze of his silent companions. All remained quiet trying to understand the grandiose and wonderfully crazy idea. Roger, Brian, and John did not hesitate for a moment and joined Freddie on this adventure. They kept going for weeks, recording and rerecording each part of the song until they were perfect. "Bohemian Rhapsody" stopped being a dream and became a real song.

It was genius.

"You're crazy!" the scandalized producer shouted. "It's impossible to launch such a long song into the market. No radio station will ever broadcast it!"

But in the morning, someone sent the song to the radios and then it happened:

the band reigned.

"Bohemian Rhapsody" played all over the world. Freddie's voice made its way into millions of people's hearts. Queen became a legend, and Freddie taught us his unique truth: life exists to be lived.

Polaroid

Queen photographed their
adventures with a Polaroid camera.

In their beginnings, they sold outlandish clothes and works of art in Kensington Market

The glamour of the stars in the wings

Queen and David Bowie collaborating on the song "Under Pressure"

Freddie discovered the "bottomless mic" when he accidentally broke the base off his microphone stand in a concert

The band in 1975

At first the band was criticized for the way they dressed.

Freddie Mercury dared to wear all kinds of clothing to try to push the show even further.

"I'm having fun with my clothes on stage. It's not a concert you're seeing. It's a fashion show."

—FREDDIE MERCURY

Freddie's passion for all things Japanese led him to wear a kimono (1976)

Harlequin outfit (1977)

Eventually, Freddie cut his long mane and let his mustache grow (early 1980s)

In the music video for the song "I Want to Break Free," the entire band dressed as women. In Britain, cross-dressing was considered a comedic tradition. But in the United States at the time, people did not take it well, and the music video was banned from being played on TV. (1984)

QUEEN STUDIO ALBUMS

★ **Queen** (1973)

★ **Queen II** (1974)

★ **Sheer Heart Attack** (1974)

★ **A Night at the Opera** (1975)

★ **A Day at the Races** (1976)

★ **News of the World** (1977)

★ **Jazz** (1978)

★ The Game (1980)

★ Flash Gordon (1980)

★ Hot Space (1982)

★ The Works (1984)

★ A Kind of Magic (1986)

★ The Miracle (1989)

★ Innuendo (1991)

★ Made in Heaven (1995)

LEARN MORE ABOUT THE HISTORY OF MUSIC WITH THESE GREAT BOOKS.

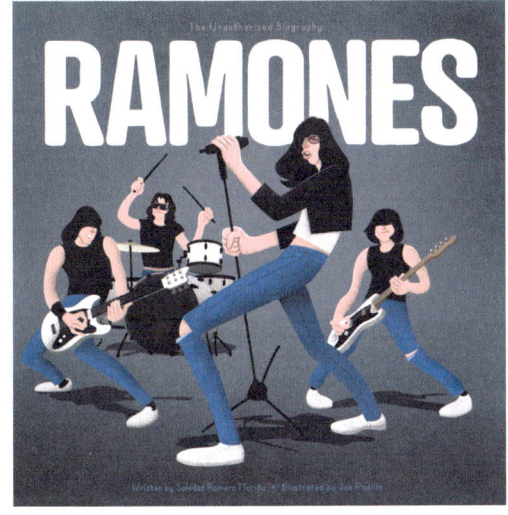

The incredible story of four friends who became legends of punk rock.

The electrifying adventure of the band that challenged metal's limits.

The origin of the band that conquered the world with electronic music.

Scan here to listen to Queen's first two LPs

First published in the United States in 2020 by Sourcebooks
Text © 2019, 2020 by Soledad Romero Mariño
Illustrations © 2019, 2020 by Laura Castelló
Cover design by Brittany Vibbert/Sourcebooks
Internal design by Will Riley
Cover and internal design © 2020 by Sourcebooks

Published by Sourcebooks eXplore, an imprint of Sourcebooks Kids
P.O. Box 4410, Naperville, Illinois 60567-4410
(630) 961-3900
sourcebookskids.com

Originally published as Band Records: *Queen* in 2019 by Reservoir Kids, an imprint of Penguin
Random House Grupo Editorial.

Library of Congress Cataloging-in-Publication Data is on file with the publisher.

Source of Production: PrintPlus Limited, Shenzhen, Guangdong Province, China
Date of Production: April 2020
Run Number: 5017105

Printed and bound in China.
PP 10 9 8 7 6 5 4 3 2 1

Queen II

SIDE A

1. Procession
2. Father to Son
3. White Queen (As It Began)
4. Some Day One Day
5. The Loser in the End